WALKING
SHORTS

Mark Richards

CONTENTS

CHAPTER ONE

INTRODUCTION

One Saturday morning in January I published one of these short stories – *The Frog on the Moor* – on Facebook, in the Walk 1,000 Miles group. 'That might make a few people laugh,' I thought, and went off to walk the dog.

When I came back my notifications had exploded. Everyone had enjoyed it. Someone had woken her husband up so she could read the story to him. I published two or three others and the reaction was the same – and it slowly dawned on me that it might be a good idea to put all the walking stories I had into a short book.

So here's the book – and it's dedicated to those members of the Walk 1,000 Miles group who've been kind enough to read the stories on a Saturday morning and be so supportive with their feedback. Thank you.

The stories are largely taken from the weekly newspaper column/blog that I've written since 2003. It starts with Alex and I walking through the woods together – when I was as far away from a 'serious walker' as it's possible to be – and ends with us plotting our second walking holiday: 6 days and 100 miles in July this year.

The book charts my journey from total walking sceptic to someone who, "high on the cliffs on the Cleveland Way, watching a snowy owl make one last, lazy reconnaissance flight over a field, gazing south to Flamborough Head and north towards Robin Hood's Bay, realised that I'd fallen in love with walking."

Walking Shorts is a collection of 25 short stories. Most of them will (hopefully!) make you laugh: one or two might make you think. As usual, serious, seasoned walkers will be horrified by some of my mistakes. The whole book is just under 20,000 words – a necessary condition of being in Amazon's 'short reads' category.

If you've read 'Father, Son and the Pennine Way' five or six of the stories might be familiar to you – but I've used my original columns here, not the slightly amended ones that appeared in the book.

But I won't waste any more of my 20,000 words. Thank you for buying *Walking Shorts*: I hope you enjoy it.

CHAPTER TWO

DANCES WITH WOLVES

*This one was written in the summer of 2013, when
Alex was just coming up to 15 – and when I realised
that he genuinely liked walking with his dad…*

From time to time I like to check that I'm alive. Gentle, reflective strolls on the beach are all very well, but sometimes I need to remind myself that I could once run a half-marathon in a respectable time. And lay the ghosts of 31st March 2006 to rest…

So today was the day. Start at the bottom of Raincliffe Woods and walk straight to the top. 15 minutes of almost continuous climbing. Twenty years ago it would have been a training run but three children and far too long at the keyboard have taken their toll.

But let's do this. The sun is shining, the dog is straining at the leash and Lucozade Sport is on special offer at the corner shop.

"Come on," I said to the official timekeeper. "Are you going to time me on your phone?"

"On my watch," Alex replied.

"Does it have a timer?"

"No, Dad. I'm going to use it to reflect the sun onto a tree-trunk and make a sundial." Teenage sarcasm. Always the best motivator.

Blimey the first part was steep. Was it this steep last year? Too early to be puffing and panting – especially as Alex and the dog were disappearing into the distance.

Ah, a brief flat bit. Thank you, God.

"Five minutes," Alex shouted from somewhere up ahead. "Keep going."

I increased my pace and rounded a bend. There was my son. And my dog – amusing herself in a spectacularly muddy stream. Should have brought the wife's car…

And now I was at the serious part. The final climb. Time to sort the men from the boys. But where was the boy? Up ahead. A long way up ahead. But the dog was keeping me company. Throw a stick? You must be joking, Pepper.

"Come on, Dad," Alex yelled. "You can beat your record."

Surely not. 15:36? The one record to rule them all?

"Come on, Dad. Sprint up the last bit."

With a mighty effort I hurled myself up the last 50 yards of the hill. And collapsed. "Urrrggghhh. Water. Quickly."

"Awesome, Dad. Just awesome."

"What – was – it?" I gasped.

"Fourteen, thirty-three. You smashed it."

"But." Gasp. "That means." Bigger gasp. "I didn't need to run."

"That's right. I lied to you. But look at your time."

And that's what you get for making babies with a psychologist.

But I was elated. Slowly my breathing returned to normal. And life in the old dog yet. Fitter than ever. Still time for some more children. We'd be home in an hour. 'Here's a tenner, Alex. Take yourself off to the pictures…'

Sadly I was rather too elated. The old dog was about to perform a new trick.

"Down here," I said to Alex when we'd walked along the top path, drunk – in my case – a gallon of water and it was finally time to head back. "Haven't been on this path for years. Take care. It's a bit tricky but you should be OK."

"It's steep, Dad…" he said, kicking a stone and watching it tumble twenty feet in front of us.

"Hang on to a branch like I'm doing."

"I'm OK. I'm fine." And with the sureness of youth he picked his way down the slope. Ah well. He'd learn. Hanging onto a branch was definitely the safest way.

Until it broke off in your hand.

There was a split-second when I thought I could stay on my feet. Then I was on my back. Sliding down the hill. Faster. Nothing to grab onto. Sliding even faster. I bounced off something. A tree stump? And stopped.

Not because of a tree stump. Bccausc Alex had grabbed a handful of my t-shirt as I slid past him.

"Impressive, Dad. Just like in a disaster movie."

I climbed gingerly to my feet. I was covered in mud. Blood trickled down my arm. Several parts of my body were arguing about which one hurt the most.

To his credit Alex didn't start laughing until he was sure I was alright. "I assume that looked pretty funny?"

"Exceptional. But you're too old to do your own stunts, Dad."

We walked slowly back to the car. The movie theme continued. "It's not a disaster movie is it?" I said. "It's a survival movie."

"You mean this is the moment when the wolves start circling…"

"Yeah. The moment I make the heroic speech. 'Save yourself, son. Leave me here. You and Pepper go on without me.'"

"Not today, Dad. You've got the car keys."

The question of my self-sacrifice having been put to one side I finally made it through the front door.

25 years ago my wife would have rushed to massage soothing balms into my battered body. She

may even have sponged my injuries as I soaked in the bath.

But we've had three children since then.

"You're filthy," she said. And you're bleeding. Don't drip blood onto the new carpet." She sniffed the air. "And the dog's rolled in fox poo. Give her a bath before you go in the shower. Or take her in with you…"

CHAPTER THREE

THE BOY WHO UNDERSTOOD WOMEN

Two years later, Alex is coming up to 17 and we're
discussing slightly more mature themes…

Alex and I are in the woods. Another dog walk, another roll in fox poo.

There's no smell quite like it is there? The first time Pepper did it she compounded the felony by rolling on the car seat. In the end the only answer was to sell the car…

But enough of my troubles. Here comes a fellow dog-walker. With wife and disappointingly well-behaved Labrador.

"Morning," I say.

The fellow dog-walker looks at me. He clearly wants to say something. The concentrated expression on his face suggests it's going to be profound. Am I about to learn one of life's great secrets? Is God finally compensating me for the fox poo?

He looks at his watch. His brain whirrs. "No," he finally says. "It's afternoon."

"I hate that," Alex says when Confucius and wife are safely out of earshot. "I mean, you're not actually saying, 'Hello, I'd just like to confirm it's not yet 12 o'clock' are you?"

"Nope. It's more, 'I greet you as a fellow dog-walker and offer you the chance to return the greeting' – if you want to get intellectual about it."

We talk some more about what you say, what you mean and the pedants who point out the difference.

I'm impressed by my son's insight. So impressed that I suggest a more in-depth discussion when we reach the top of the hill. On that nice bench. Where I can get my breath back.

"There's a book you ought to read," I say. "It's called *Men are from Mars, Women are from Venus*."

"I've heard of that…"

"Yep. It's all about how men say one thing and women hear something completely different."

"Like you and Mum?"

"Yeah, sometimes. Like I might say, 'Gosh, the kitchen's a bit untidy.'"

"And Mum thinks you're criticising her?"

"Yes. Exactly. And all I'm really doing is observing. I'm saying, 'the kitchen's untidy' like I might say 'it's raining.'

"But you don't actually tidy it up."

"Well, no. Not if there's football on TV. There's another chapter in the book," I continue, not entirely sure that the discussion is moving in my intended direction. "It's called 'Mr Fixit' or something like that."

"It's not about DIY is it?"

"No. The book's about men and women not understanding each other."

"So do you understand Mum?"

Well there's a question after twenty years of marriage. But a chance to impart some wisdom. *You understand me so well, Alex,* she'll sigh. *All thanks to my dad, darling…*

"When we started seeing each other your mum lent me a book. There was a sentence in it: 'the average man understands the average woman less well than the average Chinaman understands the average pygmy.' I don't suppose you're allowed to say that these days. Not politically correct. But it's absolutely right. I tell you, Alex, I'm certain I understand women better than the majority of men - "

"Yes, that's what Mum says…"

Was that sarcasm? I let it pass.

" – But I barely understand them at all. I used to be a real Mr Fixit. She'd come in, start telling me her problems and I'd be right there with the answers. Do this, do that, sack her, send him to Aberdeen. When really - "

"All she wanted was someone to listen."

"Yeah." What had he just said? "What did you just say'?"

"She just wanted you to listen."

"Yes. That's what it says in the book. How did you know?"

"Well, it's obvious."

"No it wasn't. Not to me. Not to 99% of men. I thought Mum wanted my advice."

"No, Dad," he said gently. "She wanted to dump her problems. Express her frustration."

Did my son instinctively understand that? Instinctively understand women? Could he sail through life without his dad's advice?

Was that possible…

CHAPTER FOUR

THE THROES OF PASSION

Sunday morning. This was too early to be awake, even for mid-summer. I fumbled for my phone. 4:04.

Why was I awake at 4:04 on a Sunday morning? Because the cat was trying to knock our bedroom door down.

I lay in bed, listened to the cat clawing frantically at the door and asked myself the obvious question. Would my wife wake up and deal with it?

She rolled over in bed, stole some more quilt off me, sighed a contented sigh and gave me an emphatic, unconscious two fingers.

So I stumbled out of bed and opened the bedroom door.

Job done, the cat brushed against my leg and trotted off happily to sleep on the bathroom floor. "No," I said to the dog. "Just no. It is nowhere near breakfast time."

I went back to bed. A pointless exercise. Is there anything more irritating in human life than lying awake listening to the person you married snoring gently?

"Sod it," I said to the dog fifteen minutes later. "Let's go. It'll soon be sunrise. At least you'll win the First Dog on the Beach award."

The holiday season. So we had to drive to the other side of town to find some beach my walking buddy was allowed on. "Calm down," I said as we came to the slipway and Pepper yelped expectantly. "Just let me park the car."

But what was that? Had I glimpsed something on the beach? Something at the bottom of the slipway?

Had a seal been washed up? Pepper face-to-face with a seal: that should be interesting.

Then a chilling thought struck me. The proverbial early morning dog walker. I could see the headlines.

Local man finds mutilated body washed up on beach.

But we were supposed to be decorating Alex's bedroom today. Would my wife accept 'helping the police with their enquiries' as a valid reason not to be back in time to strip wallpaper? Probably not…

I parked the car and opened the boot. Pepper leapt out, wagging her tail furiously. I still wasn't fully awake but it was a beautiful morning. The sun just rising out of the sea, wisps of early morning mist hovering over the beach. I took Pepper's lead and we walked towards the slipway.

And heard a noise. "What was that?" I said. "It definitely sounded like a seal."

Pepper stopped for a contemplative poo.

"That's right," I said, "The middle of the road is always a good place for a dump."

I did what was required with the poo bag – memo to self, leave the left-over curry out of the dog's reach – and headed for the bin. There was the noise again. I was finally awake – and now I could see the newspaper headline clearly.

Hero dog walker rescues stranded seal pup.

And then the seal said something.

"Oh God, yes. Harder. Right there…"

It wasn't a seal.

Which of us in our youth has not felt the urge for a little *al fresco* hanky panky? A beautiful morning, a deserted beach, low tide, young love… What could possibly go wrong?

A Springer Spaniel that's what.

Pepper – making the perfectly reasonable assumption that the young lady's cries of passion meant she was in possession of a bag of Bonios – bounded over to join in the fun.

I drew level with them. There was only one option: play the English Gentlemen. "Good morning," I said. "Looks like a lovely day. The sun should burn off this mist."

Astonishingly they seemed totally uninterested in discussing the weather.

I did the decent thing and hurled Pepper's ball fifty yards into the distance. "Come on," I said. "I don't want to be in the newspapers."

Couple's romantic tryst ruined by pervert dog walker…

CHAPTER FIVE

THEY MUST BE MAD

This one was written in the Autumn of 2015, just after Alex had started at Sixth-Form College.

A Sunday morning. My two eldest children away at university, the youngest one fast asleep. My beautiful wife next to me in bed…

Very gently, I start to kiss the back of her neck. She sighs in her sleep. Moves closer to me. I trail my hand lightly over…

…the cheese.

Tough luck. Fantasy over, mate.

You're a dad. That's all there is to it.

Think about something else and get on with making those sandwiches.

There I was, banging on the door of the corner shop while it was still pitch black. But two large cheese and

ham later I was ready. And so was Alex, my youngest
son.

"Have you got everything?"

"Yes."

"Water bottle? Waterproof trousers? Your phone?"

"Dad, [insert lengthy teenage sigh and pained expression] how many expeditions have you been on?"

"Well, technically, none. None that involved 15 miles, that's for sure."

So I keep quiet. And hand Alex his pack-out. The aforementioned sandwiches, fruit, a week's supply of chocolate. That should keep a teenage boy going until lunchtime.

"Let's go, then."

And at 7:30 on Sunday morning, we set off. Out into the wilds for the first practice expedition. Duke of Edinburgh Gold Award. And as it's a new school they need to check the kids can walk in a straight line.

It's cold, it's dark, it's drizzling.

My wife? She's standing shivering on the doorstep bidding her husband and son a tearful farewell. Or still asleep in a warm bed. You decide…

We head off towards the North York Moors, steadily climbing. The drizzle turns to rain. The early morning mist turns to fog. Or low cloud. Civilization and its trappings – warm bed, bacon sandwich – are just a distant memory. Turn left, turn right. Further into the heart of the Moors…

"Look for a lay-by before a bridge, Dad."

…And we finally arrive. Miraculously the rain has stopped, the fog has lifted. Alex could be in for a lovely day.

And he's not alone. The lay-by is packed with parked cars. I shake my head. "Are all these people out for a day's walking? It's October. They must be mad…"

"See you at four," I add and head back home. I pass a sign pointing to a North Yorkshire village. Fryup, 2 miles.

Yes please.

The sun disappears and I'm back in the fog. With Alex doing the Gold there'll be plenty more expeditions in desolate places. 'It's best to rely on parents for lifts' trills the school handout. Thanks for that.

Damn it. There should be some recognition for dads. 18 months from now my son will be at Buckingham Palace eating cucumber sandwiches and discussing Ordnance Survey maps with HRH. I'll be at home totting up the mileage.

Four o'clock came. Once again I was rudely jolted back into the real world. I switched the football off and went to collect my son. Back through the rain and fog to the lay-by before the bridge.

"All OK?"

"Yeah, it was good. Fog? No. Not when we got up on the hills. It was a really good day. You should try it some time."

"I don't think so," I said. "15 miles across the Moors? You've got me confused with someone else."

But later that year I opened a file on my computer. It was called, 'Sort Myself Out.' Little did I know what was coming…

CHAPTER SIX

SURVIVAL OF THE FITBIT-EST

It's raining outside. Not just raining: pouring down. It's been doing that for 24 hours. The rest of the country is being washed out to sea and the DIY fanatic next door is building something…

So I'm going out for a walk.

No, I'm not going to get wet. I'm going to get drenched. Soaked by the time I reach the pub on the corner. My coat's still wet from the dog walk and my waterproof shoes aren't anymore.

But I'm going. Because I owe it to my wife.

It's the least I can do.

Rewind the clock 24 hours. To Christmas morning. My wife hands me my last present. "Happy Christmas," she smiles.

A small parcel. Maybe six inches long. Cuboid? Is that right?

My presents so far suggest I'm a man who sits around reading, while drinking too much red wine and eating too much cheese.

Spot on. So I'm feeling pleased with life. But what can this be? I shake it. No sound.

"Read the clue," she says.

No more telling porkies about numbers. The truth will out.

Porkies? Numbers? "What is this? Something that sits on my desk and counts how many bacon sandwiches I have?"

"Nearly…"

I shake it again. Still nothing. And then a light bulb goes on above my head. "Ah… Thank you, darling. A Fitbit. I really wanted one." And who says romance is dead? I cross the room and kiss her in front of our traumatised children.

"So it'll record how many steps I take? I'll have to go the long way to the bacon sandwich shop."

"You're supposed to do 10,000 steps a day," Eleanor says.

So I'd heard. And I'd worked it out. Who had time to walk for two hours? "I won't get anywhere near that."

"Take the dog out, Dad. Fasten it to her collar."

"Awesome! Brilliant plan."

"Except it records your heart rate as well."

Damn it. Thirty minutes on the dog and all my targets would have been met…

But the Fitbit, it appeared, was my friend.

"Look at this," I said triumphantly when I'd finally set it up. "I've already used 945 calories. And I haven't eaten anything."

"Shouldn't you tell it about the chocolate twist and toast you had for breakfast?"

"I don't want to wear the batteries out. Besides, I'm checking my heart rate now."

A thought occurred to me. After more than twenty years of marriage I should have known better, but it wandered carelessly out through my mouth. "I'll need to wear it when, you know… When the children are asleep…"

I smiled seductively. Or what I fondly imagined was seductively.

"What?"

"It'll check my maximum heart rate."

"It may have escaped your attention, dearest, but I'm your wife – not a research tool." Yep, definitely a mistake.

"I've set a weight loss target," I said, desperately trying to retrieve my brownie points.

"How much?"

"Eleven kilos. Nearly two stone in old money."

"So you'll be giving up red wine and cheese?" I mentally flipped through potential New Year's resolutions. Nope, that one was definitely missing.

"I'll be exercising more," I said defiantly.

Starting now. What else could I do? Sometimes marriage demands sacrifice. This was mine: a moral duty to come home looking like I'd jumped in the sea.

I opened the front door. "Hell's bells. It's like the waterfall scene in *Last of the Mohicans*."

"Stay alive," my wife replied. "I *will* find you. No matter how wet you are…"

CHAPTER SEVEN

WAITING FOR GODOT – AND MY SON

Written in January 2016 – Alex has a part-time job…

"What time is it?" my wife asked.

"Ten to ten."

"Are you going for him or am I?"

Am I not a gentleman? Does chivalry not seep from my very pores? Yes, damn it, occasionally it does. So I was going for Alex.

Besides, we'd just watched *Billy Elliott*. I was in sentimental father/son mode.

"I'll go: you've had a tough week."

But when to go? That was the $64,000 question. Or in my case, the 64 minute question…

"I'm off," I said, kissing my wife. "He'll phone just as I'm parking. Perfect timing."

"You say that every week."

She's right. I do. But no, he doesn't phone while I'm driving to the hotel. No problem: I'm parked in pole position. I can see straight into the dining room. The empty dining room. Alex will be out in a minute, and very shortly afterwards I'll be in the warm and welcoming arms of my wife…

Yep, there's the waitress he works with. Claire? Coming out, phoning her dad, walking up the street to meet him. Not even worth turning the car engine off…

Hang on, who's that in the dining room? My son. Damn it. What's he doing? Moving a table. Laying the table – for breakfast. Sigh. Could be another ten minutes. Engine off. Start shivering.

Not long, I text to my wife. *Dining room is empty. Don't fall asleep.*

Think he's just finishing off, I text five minutes later. *Definitely not long.*

The hotel door opens. Brilliant. I turn the engine on. Then I turn it off. An elderly couple come out. She's carrying a plate of sandwiches. Was a three course meal not enough for you, madam?

Someone comes back into the dining room. Alex. Again. He stares at a table.

Alex is in the dining room, I text. *He's staring at a table.*

Really, darling? That is interesting. Do I detect a hint of late night marital sarcasm?

More old people come out. Without sandwiches – but with party hats.

A lot of old people are coming out.

You do realise I could be asleep don't you? No, it's not sarcasm. Just a pressing need to go to sleep. Well I'm very sorry, wife. If I'm going to suffer you're going to suffer...

Suddenly one of the old men – yes, with party hat – taps on the car window. I reluctantly wind it down.

"Are you the taxi we ordered?"

"No," I reply through gritted teeth. "I'm the taxi my son orders. Every Saturday night."

"Ah," he said. "Is that your son? Alex? The waiter? A fine young man."

Parental pride sends a warm glow through me. Swiftly followed by a bucket of cold water.

"He'll not be out for a while. It's the British Legion. A few die-hards. They've just ordered some more drinks."

This is like 'Waiting for Godot...' I texted.

Godot never turned up.

Another half-hour. Do you want me to keep you updated?

Only if you want to sleep in the garage.

...From which I judge that my wife doesn't want to pursue our fascinating conversation. I glance at my watch. Sorry, at my Fitbit. I'm still not used to seeing it on my wrist.

I press the button to see the time. 10:47. And press it again. 7,787 steps.

Which means...

Which means I'm roughly 20 minutes away from getting to 10,000 steps for the first time in my life. Ten minutes down to the seafront, ten minutes back and it's mission accomplished.

But I can't. Supposing Alex comes out and I'm not here?

The answer is obvious. Laps of the Crescent. Never more than 2 minutes from the hotel.

I climb out of the car and pull my hood up. Start walking and press my Fitbit.

Supposing he comes out after ten minutes? Supposing I'm left hanging on 9,850? I'll have to wake my wife up to tell her I'm just walking down to the corner shop…

Take your time, British Legion. The Holy Grail is in sight.

Providing I could cope with the boredom. Three laps, four, five. Up the hill, past the flats, past the hotel, down the hill, past the Art Gallery, start again, up the hill…

It happens on my sixth lap. Right outside Scarborough's Art Gallery. My Fitbit suddenly starts buzzing and vibrating. There's no other way to describe it. The little fella's having an orgasm, right there on my left wrist.

"Sorry, Dad," Alex says. "There was a party. British Legion. Claire and I tossed for it. I lost. Still," he adds cheerfully, "It's another hour's pay. Have you been OK?"

"I've found the Holy Grail," I say, and ignore my son's baffled expression…

CHAPTER EIGHT

ONE DAD, ONE SON, ONE VERY LONG WALK

This one – and the five stories that follow it – were written through the spring and early summer of 2016, as Alex and I prepared for our five days on the Pennine Way

It may be the stupidest thing I've ever done.

Or it might just be the best…

I've invited Alex out for a walk. Quite a long walk…

Alex, I texted, *can you come downstairs when you're ready. I want to put an idea to you.*

Let me explain. I need to do something physical. I want a challenge. And I want to do it before my left knee decides the only thing it's good for is a waiting list.

So I've had an idea. A walk with my son. After all, we have our best conversations when we're out walking the dog.

But I'm planning something a little longer. Five days on the Pennine Way. Maybe 80 miles. Sometime in the summer holidays…

Yes, of course I have doubts. I used to be really fit. But that was 20 years ago. The occasional glass of wine and the odd plate of cheese have passed my lips since then. The furthest I've walked is about five miles. At walking the dog pace.

But my worries are nothing to the outright scepticism I'll face from the family. I can hear it now…

"Dad, every time you try to do something physical you get injured."

"No, I don't."

"Yes, you do. You fell down that bank in the woods. And what about the time you tried to race Eleanor up those sand-dunes?"

"Tore his hamstring." My beloved will tick off the gory details…

"Or that time you tried to show off at football?"

"Tore his ankle ligaments."

"Damn it, you can put your back out emptying the dishwasher."

"That's not strictly accurate, darling. Your dad can put his back out by sneezing as well. Or doing something *really* dangerous like putting his socks on."

Someone was coming downstairs. Alex. "Any pudding?"

"Just put your stomach on hold for five minutes. I want to ask you something. You and your mum.

…So I have this plan," I explained. "I want to do a physical challenge. Before I'm too old. And something with Alex. Before the last of my children leaves home."

"Spit it out, Dad."

"I'd like to go for a walk. On the Pennine Way. Five days. Maybe eighty miles. And I'd like you to come with me."

Five days alone with his dad. Just what every 17 year old boy has at the top of his wish list.

Beverley and Alex looked at me. Here it came…

"That's great," my son said. "Let's do it."

"Brilliant," my wife said. "Go for it."

"Are you sure?"

"Yeah. I like walking with you, Dad."

As simple as that. And the die is cast. Some time in August my son and I are going to lace up our walking boots. Beverley will drive us to Middleton-in-Teesdale. We'll head south towards the Tan Hill Inn, Hawes, Malham and Gargrave. Five days, five packs of blister plasters and 81 miles later we'll reach Thornton in Craven.

I have no idea if I can do it. But I've made a commitment to my son – and to my ego – and I've five months to get myself fit. It'll mean saying goodbye to a few old friends. No red wine between Monday and

Friday. And no cheese – sadly between Monday and Monday.

But there'll be compensations. I'll be reunited with several pairs of jeans whose sole purpose at the moment is to mock me.

Not that I'll be walking in jeans. No way. We're going to do this properly. "I'll need some of those Bear Grylls survival trousers."

"Darling, you're walking through North Yorkshire. Not the Borneo jungle."

My wife was right. I crossed 'machete' off the list…

For those of you that have read 'Father, Son and the Pennine Way' that was the original plan. I wanted to walk north to south – Middleton to Thornton-in-Craven – for no other reason than I thought I'd get a better tan walking south. Then I discovered that the baggage transport companies only did south to north…

THE SCOUTING TRIP

One part holiday: one part scouting mission for the Pennine Way expedition. My beloved and I were in the Dales for two days, the house – and the continued survival of the pets – left confidently with Ellie and Alex.

Everything's fine. Stop worrying, they texted.

Sadly, my reconnaissance wasn't going as well.

"Where's the OS map?" Beverley asked as we said a damp goodbye to Hardraw Force and headed further into the Yorkshire Dales.

Ah. *That's* why I'd had a nagging, something-left-behind feeling all morning…

"In the bedroom."

"You've left it behind?"

"As it's not currently hanging round my neck, yes."

That seemed one of the less attractive aspects of walking. The average walker has more junk round his neck than I had when I was 20 and going through my Thai love beads phase.

I pointed the car at the Tan Hill Inn – the highest pub in the country and, as I was eventually to discover, the only one with its own snowplough – and began to get cold feet.

"What is it?" Beverley asked as I pulled off the road and stared at an endless succession of hills.

"I'm beginning to feel…"

"What?"

"Daunted. The words 'bitten off more than you can chew' keep going through my head."

"You said you wanted a physical challenge."

"I know. I just hadn't realised it was going to be *this* physical. Every signpost that says, 'Pennine Way' points straight up a hill."

I was also realising that strolling along the beach wondering when I could wear my shorts wasn't adequate training. And that I'd need a serious pair of walking boots.

"How much?" I said to a man in a shop.

"Hundred and fifty," he replied cheerfully.

"Gulp," I said.

But consolation wasn't far away. We finally made it back to our B&B. I decanted my wife into the shower and went back to the car for the shopping.

"Not going to the pub tonight?" It was Chris, the owner, stealing five minutes with the evening sun.

"No, just bread and cheese in the room." And a bottle of red wine, obviously. Sadly, one of us had stayed on the diet and self-discipline wagon. One of us hadn't so much fallen off as jumped willingly.

"Do you like your cheese?"

Possibly the easiest question I've ever been asked. "One of our regulars is a cheesemaker. He makes this astonishing Stilton. Do you want to try it?"

Well, well, well. Who would have thought it? The Dark Lord himself, sitting quietly outside a B&B in the Yorkshire Dales. And here I was being tempted…

"Yes, please. And could I take some for Beverley? She loves Stilton."

"I can't possibly eat that much," the woman who loved Stilton said two minutes later.

"Can't you, darling?" I said innocently. And downstairs the Dark Lord chuckled and added another one to the lost souls column…

I made up for it the next morning by marching up to Middleham Moor to watch impossibly beautiful racehorses. If it was good enough for Derby winners it was good enough for me. An hour striding purposefully across the Moor should burn enough calories for a full English.

Ah. Another problem. Soft going. Very wet going to be more precise. My left heel squelched ominously. Swiftly followed by its mate on the right.

"I'll have to buy those boots," I said to Beverley. "My waterproof shoes are waterproof no longer."

"Leave them in the hall to dry out. Just don't forget them."

"Don't be ridiculous," I said. "As if an experienced Dalesman like me would leave his walking shoes behind."

"Oh," I said when we were 40 miles down the A1.

"What's the matter?" my wife asked.

"You remember the map…"

CHAPTER TEN

THE DIE IS CAST

Written on 1ˢᵗ May 2016

That's it, then. No backing out now. Exactly three months from today Beverley will decant Alex and I at the River House Hotel in Malham. We'll eat a hearty evening meal, an even heartier breakfast and then we'll start walking.

Five days and 80 miles later she'll collect a bedraggled husband and a what-was-all-the-fuss-about son from Dufton – 13 miles outside Penrith and the end of our Pennine Way journey.

I've booked all the B&Bs. I've paid the deposits. So there's no backing out. Especially as Alex tells me he's "looking forward to it, Dad."

As I wrote a few weeks ago, I want to do a physical challenge 'before my left knee decides the only thing it's good for is a waiting list.' There's the small matter of some father/son time before Alex goes to university next year.

But there's also the rather larger matter of my own fears. In no particular order these are:

Is my body up to the physical challenge? Yes, I've lost weight. Yes, I've re-discovered several old pals in the wardrobe. But 40 minutes on the beach at lunchtime does not equal five days on the Pennine Way.

And over the last ten years I'd conveniently forgotten about my groin: specifically the adductor muscle therein. It sent me a postcard on Saturday morning 'Remember me?' Playing football with the dog I turned sharply.

"Why is that man lying on the beach, Mummy?" I heard a child say.

Will I be able to keep up with Alex? He walks faster on his D of E expeditions with an SAS pack on his back than I walk on the beach with a phone in my pocket. Will it be like the time I went running with Ellie and she waited on the corner turning cartwheels until I caught up?

Will we still be friends? Alex and I have a great relationship. Some of my best moments as a dad have been the long, rambling, philosophical conversations we've had as we've walked the dog. But five days for a teenage boy? One on one with his dad? With his increasingly-knackered, possibly wet, probably bad-tempered dad? In a part of the world where 'intermittent' will be considered a success for the mobile phone network? As the nation's sports pundits like to say, it's a big ask...

And then there's the cost. 'I'll do a bit of walking,' I thought. 'How expensive can that be?'

I've already recounted the uplifting conversation with the man in the shop. Spend anything less than £150 on boots and my feet will apparently be underwater for five days.

Waterproof jacket. Waterproof trousers – those sexy ones you can unzip and turn into shorts, obviously. But I have far more to worry about than my trousers...

"You'll need a hat, Dad."

"What? I look like a knob in a hat." I turned to my wife. "Tell him I don't need a hat."

"Your father's right, Alex. By the end of day five he'll be wearing a red t-shirt, those mustard shorts he bought because he knew they'd annoy me, blue socks and muddy boots. He won't need a hat to look like a knob."

"Protection from the sun, Dad. And mosquitoes," my son added cheerfully. "And supposing we get lost? We could be roaming the Dales in search of human habitation."

I doubted that. If I knew my son he wouldn't be roaming far from breakfast, lunch and dinner. But better be on the safe side. "OK, you can be navigator.

Or whatever walkers call it. I suppose that means we need a compass?"

The list of what we needed grow'd like Topsy. I could see the inevitable appointment at the bank all too clearly.

"I need an overdraft."

"Certainly, sir. What for?"

"I'm going for a walk…"

CHAPTER ELEVEN

FALLING IN LOVE ON THE CLEVELAND WAY

This was written around the same time, and published on the North York Moors website. It was for a new audience, which explains the two or three instances of repetition.

Let me introduce myself: or let me introduce the man I was 14 months ago.

105.4kg. If you still think in old money, that's 16st 8lbs. A wardrobe full of clothes, 75% of which had mysteriously become too small for me. Walking? Yes, I walked the dog on the cliff top three of four times a week – after all, we live on the north side of Scarborough, the cliff top is five minutes away.

But serious walking? Don't be ridiculous. That was for people with backpacks, haggard faces and a healthy collection of knee supports.

And then my wife gave me a Fitbit for Christmas. It politely suggested I do 10,000 steps a day. I snorted in derision: on my first day back at work I managed 3,874. Stories filtered through of a friend doing 17,000 steps a day: I dismissed them as the stuff of fantasy.

But gradually, I made changes: parked the car at the far end of the car park, abandoned my lunchtime sandwich and went for a walk. And one night in January, as I waited to collect Alex from his part-time job, I found the Holy Grail. 10,000 steps – and with a few exceptions, it's been 10,000 steps ever since.

And the weight was coming off: the vast majority of my clothes were still out of bounds, but maybe my belt wasn't under quite the pressure it had been…

Winter gave way to spring – and the 'cliff top' ceased to exist. "If you don't mind" I said to my wife, "We serious walkers call it the Cleveland Way."

Gradually, my walks were becoming longer: which was just as well – because I'd invited my youngest son for a walk. Alex is 17: I wanted to spend some father/son time with him before he went to university. And I wanted to do a physical challenge before I became too old for a physical challenge.

"So how about it?" I said. "Five days and 80 miles on the Pennine Way. One week in the summer holidays?"

"Sure," he said, "Why not?"

He was a veteran of Duke of Edinburgh expeditions. I wasn't – and now I was back on the Cleveland Way training seriously.

…And meeting Denis Malcolm Kendal.

I've reached the age now where I think about how I'd like to be remembered. Denis Malcolm Kendal is a plaque on a seat. He was only 69 when he died, but now he sits on the Cleveland Way, gazing out to Denmark. He sees the sun rise every morning, watches the gulls circling and has just the right number of walkers to keep him company.

That seems a decent memorial to me.

"See you next week, Denis," I said and carried on walking north – as I did every Sunday.

And on one of those Sunday mornings, high on the cliffs above Hayburn Wyke, watching a snowy owl make one last, lazy reconnaissance flight over a field, gazing south to Flamborough Head and north towards Robin Hood's Bay, I realised something very simple.

I'd fallen in love with walking.

Standing there, the early morning sun glinting off a flat sea, a paddleboarder gliding past on his way to Whitby, I realised how much I loved the solitude and the stillness: the time to reflect – and the sheer joy of being outside and active while the rest of the world was stumbling downstairs to breakfast.

Not just the solitude and the stillness: I loved the romance and the mystery of walking – especially the place names on the Ordnance Survey map. I didn't park the car at Burniston Rocks any more; I parked it at Crook Ness. The dog and I marched past Flat Scar and Long Nab and the Sailors' Grave.

And every Sunday morning we walked past the old coastguard hut. A few hundred yards north of Crook Ness and, like Denis, staring resolutely out to sea. It's used for birdwatching now, finally de-commissioned after the Second World War.

Spent the war in that coastguard hut did your Grandad. Set off every morning with his flask and his ham sandwiches. Five years waiting for Adolf's battleships to come over the horizon.

He should have been there a thousand years earlier. He'd have seen Thorgils Skarthi and his band of Viking raiders – who also fell in love with the view, and founded Scarborough.

"Come on," I said to Pepper, "Another mile and then we'll turn round. And don't worry – we'll be back next week…"

CHAPTER TWELVE

BOOTS ON THE GROUND

I've gone through my whole life without being remotely interested in footwear with brand names like 'Mountain Goat' or 'Crag Climber.'

But this walking lark has changed everything.

With the Pennine Way now just an ominous seven weeks away my thoughts have turned to my feet. And the simple fact that I'll need something more than my trainers to march up Pen-y-Ghent and its friends.

The same goes for Alex. He finished his Duke of Edinburgh practice expedition with his feet inside plastic bags. His boots took a week to dry out. So they'll shortly be on first name terms with a skip.

He needs new boots. I need new boots. But 'this walking lark' is not cheap.

My original train of thought – 'This sounds like fun. Fresh air. Testing myself. Stunning views. Agreeable lunch in the pub. Yep, I'll just lace up my trainers and pop outside' has given way to grim reality. The list of what I need is long and growing longer. We're not quite at the Eleanor-goes-to-university level, but we're getting there.

And top of that list is boots.

Fortunately, help is at hand. Hi-Tec has ridden – or marched – to the rescue. Our boots are to be sponsored. And here we are trying them on. Eat your heart out, Mountain Goats. I'm now in love with a pair of Altitude PRO RGS boots.

How cool is that? Three months ago I was an overweight middle aged bloke that drank too much red wine and ate too much cheese. Now I have boots with more go-faster initials than my car.

Let's see how they feel…

There's something remarkably stupid about testing a pair of walking boots by strolling round the shop. Carpets have an irritating habit of being level. And three steps up a wooden plank doesn't quite equal climbing remorselessly for two hours. But what else can you do?

Look, mate, I just need to go and walk five miles in these if that's OK. I'll leave my son as security.

'I'll ask the manager, sir, but I think it's against company policy to take hostages.'

But maybe I don't need to. Because the boots are propelling me forwards. Wowzer. Suddenly I'm Jack the Giant Killer striding around in his seven league boots. Two hours remorseless climbing? Bring it on.

"Right, boots sorted," I said to Alex. "We just need a few other things…"

'A few other things' was a remarkable understatement.

I still didn't own any of those sexy trousers that unzip and turn into shorts. Neither did I have a hat. See the earlier discussion: I look ridiculous in a hat, but I'll look even more ridiculous with a bright red neck. What else? A lifetime's supply of blister plasters – and the assorted requirements for battling mother nature and her smaller flying creatures.

"Anything else, Dad? Padded jacket? Rope? Gaiters?"

"What?"

"Gaiters. They go over your ankles and stop everything getting muddy."

"I'm planning to do this walk in style, Alex. Not look like some Victorian explorer trying to find Dr. Livingstone."

"Extra fleece, Dad? Thermal vest?"

"Alex, how many times? We are going in the first week of August. We'll be walking through the sun-kissed Yorkshire Dales. The only decision will be factor 8 or factor 10."

"Inflatable canoe?"

My son, showing that revising for his Law exam had not dulled the edge of sarcasm…

Then I saw him staring fixedly into a cabinet.

Alex was looking at a machete. Next to it was a knife that must have been on Freddie Kruger's wish list. So becoming a mass murderer was quite easy. All you had to do was wander in for some mozzy repellent and murmur, "Oh, yes. I almost forgot…"

"I don't think we'll be needing one of those, Alex."

"Can't be too sure, Dad. Remember you'll be leaving Yorkshire. Crossing the border. County Durham – into enemy territory…"

CHAPTER THIRTEEN

21 DAYS AND COUNTING

It was the end of February. *Can you come downstairs? I want to put an idea to you.* I texted to Alex. *I want to put an idea to you.*

The idea was a walk in the Dales. Five days, 80 miles on the Pennine Way.

"Sure," he said. "Why not?" And the die was cast.

…For the beginning of August. Five months to get fit. Five months of planning and preparation. A deadline which – like Christmas to a six year old – would never arrive.

Except it has.

My appointment with hills, more hills and a pair of walking boots is less than three weeks away. I've been training since March. I'd like to tell you that I'm as brown as the proverbial nut. But where our athletes have been warming up for the Rio Olympics by sloping off to the Pyrenees, I've been on the Cleveland Way. In the fog.

And yes, perilously close to the edge a few times…

Anyway, here's the progress report since my youngest son said 'yes' and started my love affair with Kendal Mint Cake.

I've lost 10.5kg. I've walked 913 miles. That's from Scarborough to Berlin. Another five months and I'll be in Latvia.

And I've discovered something about myself. I know you'll keep it to yourself so I'll 'fess up.

I'm frightened of walking downhill.

More specifically, I'm frightened of walking down flights of steps: old, weathered stone ones. Of which there are plenty on my stretch of the Cleveland Way. As I've managed to put my back out and spend three days in bed through the simple act of sneezing, the damage I could do to myself walking down 200 uneven and slippery steps doesn't bear thinking about.

Naturally I assumed I'd be alone in this. Another furtive little secret I'd carry to my grave.

But pop that little phobia into Google and it appears that the whole world is frightened of walking downhill. Disappointingly it doesn't have a sexy Latin name – there's bathmophobia (fear of stairs, or slopes) and basophobia, the fear of falling – but there doesn't appear to be a phobia especially for walkers.

But my goodness, I'm not alone. Half a million results on Google and counting.

At home, however, I am entirely without sympathy…

"You're frightened of walking down steps? You'd better stick to the downstairs toilet, Dad."

"…And sleep on the sofa."

"Look, I'm pushing myself to the limits. Boldly going where no man has gone before. Well, at seven o'clock on a Saturday morning, anyway. All while you lot are rotting in bed."

'Rotting in bed…' Where on earth did that come from? My dad, sadly. His regular accusation when I was a teenager. I wonder what he'd think of me now…

My children remained resolutely unimpressed. But come the next morning there I was again. Five miles from home. And, sadly, all intelligent conversation with the dog exhausted.

Time to contact my lovely wife. Not that she'd be awake yet but a quick text: a) to wake her up and b) to let her know I was still alive.

Clearly I couldn't stop to text. *Scarborough man walks over edge of cliff while texting.* At least I'd make it into the Darwin Awards.

So I dictated into my phone. I can't remember the exact words. Something about where I was, how far I'd gone, what time I expected to be home. A simple, loving message.

This is what my phone sent:

Good morning. Stop wobbling down about 10 to come home. In the long sleeve top restaurant restaurant for about 10 you slept well

Clearly when my wife received that message there were only three possible explanations:

I'd joined a secret Saturday morning drinking club

I'd plunged off the cliff top to the rocks below and – delirious with pain – had tried to send one last, loving message to my family

The phone reception on a foggy, desolate cliff top wasn't all it might be

Her reply was short and to the point. *Doesn't make much sense, but assume you're alive*

Looks like she plumped for option 3, decided not to bother air/sea rescue and went back to sleep…

CHAPTER FOURTEEN

THE HEARTY BREAKFAST

The deal was simple. I would wake Alex at 7:30. That would give us plenty of time for breakfast and we'd start walking at 9:00.

So inevitably I woke up at 5:30. Normally, that's not a problem. I am by nature one of God's early risers – and I like it that way. I go downstairs, feed the animals, drink a glass of 50/50 orange and grapefruit juice, read the news, check my e-mails and occasionally pick up my (very light) weights and definitely decide to start working out tomorrow.

And I enjoy the time to myself.

But when you're trapped in a strange bedroom it's a different story. What the hell was I going to *do* for the next two hours?

I dutifully tapped *Riverhouse1* into my iPad and read the news. *All* the news. I wrote my notes on

Malhamdale's award winning sausages and sent a text to Beverley. I read every word that had ever been written on the Malham to Horton-in-Ribblesdale section of the Pennine Way. Twice.

And I worried about whether I'd make it through the day.

Furthest distance covered in training, 12 miles. Along what I was beginning to suspect was a very easy stretch of the Cleveland Way and a very flat railway line. Had I been training for the Tour de France by cycling to the corner shop?

But we were here. And I was pleased. Pleased the waiting was over. Pleased the challenge had finally arrived. Above all, pleased I was facing it with my son.

I crept out of bed and turned the shower on. Not the best start to the day. My daughter had cried on me with more force. But I had no aches and pains. I'd come through the training. Now all I had to do was walk for five days…

I got dressed. Lucky pants… Is it just men that have lucky pants? I suspect so. I can't believe there's a woman anywhere in the world who thinks Birmingham City will avoid relegation because she's wearing blue knickers.

Anyway, lucky pants, shorts, t-shirt. And Ray Mears. Technically 'Ray' was a gilet from Mountain Warehouse. Slightly overpriced at £19.99 but it had more pockets than you could count. Phone, Kendal Mint Cake, tissues, notebook, pen, 500ml bottle of water – they all disappeared without trace and I'd barely scratched the surface.

"Ray Mears has got a jacket like that, Dad," Alex said when I first put it on. And as I think 'gilet' is about the most pretentious word in the English language, it's been 'Ray Mears' ever since.

I woke Alex. "Let's go," I said. "Cometh the hour, cometh the father and son."

But not before breakfast. The River House dining room was like the Buck last night: dark and uninspiring. And empty. "Maybe everyone else is starting later than us, Dad…"

'Everyone' was a relative term. How could there be so many 'vacancies' signs on August 1st? Five weeks earlier the UK had voted 'Leave:' the pound had plunged. The entire nation was supposed to be on staycation while tumbleweed blew along the Spanish beaches.

Whether she'd voted 'Remain' or there was some other reason, Mrs Riverhouse didn't look happy. I occasionally have a fantasy about running a B&B in an isolated beauty spot. But I suspect the reality is rather different. The constant battles with guests, suppliers and Trip Advisor must take their toll. And then along comes Airbnb to turn us all into guest houses. I made a mental note to tap 'divorce statistics for B&Bs' into Google…

Two middle-aged French women arrived. We dutifully said 'good morning' and they dutifully ordered a full English. Then they stared at it with that special expression – a mixture of awe and disgust – that the French save for a full English breakfast. But credit where le crédit is due: they ploughed through it.

If I have an occasional fantasy about running a B&B I have a permanent fantasy about breakfast in France. Sitting outside, coffee, croissants, French bread... Is the opposite true? Is there someone in Poitou-Charente waking up every morning with a secret longing for black pudding, award-winning sausages and a fried egg?

"What would you like in your sandwiches?" Breakfast was over. Now we were with Mr Riverhouse, negotiating the terms of our packed lunch.

"What are our choices?"

"Cheese or ham."

Blimey. MasterChef. I asked for one of each. At least Alex could take his pick.

"Pickle on your cheese? Dab of mustard on the ham?"

"Just a smear of mustard," I said, remembering my James Herriot. A 'dab' in the Yorkshire Dales would be uneatable to a wimp like me.

"How far are you going?" he asked.

"Dufton," I said. "Five days. The wife's picking us up on Friday afternoon. Well," I added, "Unless she's changed her mind after a week without me."

He laughed and handed me the packed lunches. We went back upstairs and Alex put them in the backpack. Our enormous orange backpack.

Another confession. I was feeling guilty about the backpack. I'd made a list of what we needed to take with us every day: then Alex had taken over and made a proper list. Now it was all in the backpack. While he was in the shower I'd casually lifted it up. I suspect the SAS invade countries with less weight on their backs.

"Are you sure?" I said again. "We can do morning and afternoon. Or an hour each."

"No," he said. "I'll do today. You carry it tomorrow."

Both Bev and I had suggested two smaller backpacks. But there was the 40 litre waterproof monster from college lying in our hall, still not returned from his D of E expedition – and with all the straps, supports and waterproof covers you could ever need. "No point wasting the money," Alex had said. So we didn't.

And now we were standing outside the River House B&B in Malham. It was time to go.

But I couldn't just start walking. "Wait a minute," I said. "I want to say something."

"What?"

I wanted to tell Alex that the day he shrugged and said, "Sure, I like walking with you" he changed my life. I wanted to say that he'd given me the chance to do something that I'd thought was impossible. That if he hadn't said 'yes' I'd still be three stone overweight with a wardrobe of clothes I couldn't wear.

I wanted to say that whatever happened over the next five days, nothing would beat that simple moment of setting off – of keeping a commitment we'd made to each other. I wanted to say that every minute of the training was worth it just to be standing outside the River House B&B with my son.

I wanted to say that just by coming with me he'd given me the most precious gift he could ever give me.

I wanted to say…

But 17 year old boys are not big on emotional speeches. Especially from their dad. So I said, "Thanks." And added, "Thanks for coming with me. Thanks for giving me the chance to do this. I'm really grateful. And I love you."

"You're welcome," my son said. And he started walking up the hill towards Malham Cove – and five days with his dad.

That was on Monday August 1st 2016. On the Friday, after 5 days and 90 miles, we arrived in Dufton. It was, very simply, the best father/son time of my life – but there were a few adventures along the way…

CHAPTER FIFTEEN

I WOULD WALK ONE THOUSAND MILES

We're now in 2017, and I've joined a group on Facebook...

I thought the walk Alex and I did on the Pennine Way was spectacular. 90 miles, 5 days. Middle aged writer, never done any previous walking. What could be more impressive?

Epic, you might say.

Only a matter of time before they decided the nation had seen enough of Bear Grylls and came knocking on my door...

Sadly, I was suffering from Red Car Syndrome.

You know the disease. You never notice red cars: but once you start to think about them they're everywhere.

Yes, I was proud of the achievement. But clearly I wasn't the only iron man around…

"Nice weekend?" I said to a vague acquaintance.

"Hectic," she said. "In Dover. My husband was swimming the channel."

"Keeping busy?" I asked an accountant I know.

"Training for an ultra-marathon," he said. "Hadrian's Wall. 69 miles in 24 hours."

And then I went on Twitter – to see that one of my followers has decided to climb every mountain in Scotland inside 12 months.

Busy day, darling?

Well I'm at the opticians first thing. Then I'm popping up Ben Nevis. But I should be back for the school run.

The UK seems to have divided neatly in two. One half is watching *Gogglebox* and ordering a pizza: the other half is cycling up Snowdon.

Clearly I can't rest on my laurels. Or on a certain part of my anatomy. I need a challenge for the summer and I'd like to do another walk with Alex. But he has his A-levels and his summer job. Not to mention the First Serious Girlfriend. Somehow I think the pull of his walking boots has dimmed a little…

I've suggested the Yorkshire Three Peaks or the Lyke Wake Walk in the hope that he'll spare me 24 hours. I'm still waiting for an answer.

So clearly it's down to me. And I duly announced my targets over the dinner table.

"I've joined this group on Facebook," I said. "I'm going to walk 1,000 miles this year."

My wife's reply was short and to the point. "Pass the gravy, will you?"

Clearly she hadn't heard me properly. Or maybe I needed to make it more exciting, more of a journey. Help my family visualise it. "That's out of our front door, turn right, and walk to Milan," I said. "Through France, Switzerland, across the Alps…"

"What about the English Channel?" Alex asked.

"Figuratively," I said.

"You probably do 1,000 miles going for extra wine and cheese every night…"

I patiently explained the difference between 'boots on' and 'boots off:' that walking would only count when it was 'boots on.' They still weren't impressed.

"So how are you doing so far?"

"As of the end of last week, 150 miles. 151.9 if you want me to be precise." My wife rolled her eyes: clearly she didn't need the specifics…

"So you've reached Nottingham?"

"Further south," I said. "Just past Leicester."

"Well you're nowhere near France – and it's already March."

I pointed out that it had been dark. And wet. That work dictated I walk in the mornings. And that manfully striding 10 miles along the cliffs wasn't the best idea when you couldn't see the edge.

"That's why I need to do something with Alex."

He didn't take the bait. "How much further do you need to walk, Dad?"

"850 miles. 20 miles a week."

"What? Every week?"

"Yes."

"Supposing you get ill? Or injured?" my wife asked.

"Yeah, Dad. Remember all those dangerous things you do. All the ways you can injure your back. Emptying the dishwasher. Getting shaved. Sneezing…"

I rose above it and went into the hall for my trainers. "Come on," I said to the dog. "Time for another two miles. We could be having breakfast at Watford Gap Services next week…"

'Boots on' I walked 1,038 miles in 2017. I reached 'Milan' on Saturday December 16th.

CHAPTER SIXTEEN

THE LONG MARCH

"Alex wants to know what to get you for your birthday." My wife, speaking – surprise, surprise – just before my birthday.

I've reached the age where I don't want things anymore. I want events, memories. What I value is someone's thought – and their time. Especially in Alex's case…

"Shall I tell you what I really want?"

"Well, duh, that's why I asked the question."

"I'd like him to do another walk with me."

For anyone that doesn't know, last year Alex and I walked 90 miles in 5 days on the Pennine Way: possibly the most rewarding five days of my life.

At the time we'd talked about doing something every year. "As long as you're up to it, Dad."

But this year has been tricky. Alex starts his A-levels on the same day that Theresa May is commanding our attendance at the polling station. So revision is at the top of his agenda.

Well, joint top... There's also Libby, the First Serious Girlfriend. Not surprisingly, a much hotter proposition than his dad, his walking boots and ten miles in persistent drizzle...

Much as I'd like to, I know that a repeat of last year's five day hike is out of the question. But maybe I could squeeze a day out of him...

"There are two I'd like to do," I said. "The Yorkshire Three Peaks Challenge and the Lyke Wake Walk. I'll send him the details."

"You'd better send them to me as well," Beverley said. "No doubt you'll be expecting me to be taxi driver and back-up crew."

I smiled, and offered her a large gin.

"There are two options," I said to Alex an hour later. "The Yorkshire Three Peaks Challenge. 24 miles in 12 hours up Ingleborough, Whernside and Pen y Ghent."

"We've already been up Pen y Ghent."

"I know. And I still remember how frightened I was. But that's why it's called a challenge."

"What's the other one?"

"The Lyke Wake Walk. 40 miles across the widest part of the North York Moors. To be completed in less than 24 hours."

"You do realise it gets dark at night, Dad?"

"Yeah. So realistically 16 hours. Unless your mum buys me a head torch for my birthday."

"Let me think about it," he said, promising nothing. "Have you sent me the links?"

I had. And he delivered his verdict on my birthday.

So mid-July will find us in Osmotherley, setting off at first light to follow the old coffin trail and walk 40 miles across the highest and widest part of the North York Moors to the coast, and the bar of the Raven Hall Hotel where – see above – our faithful road manager will be waiting for us.

And yes, 40 miles – 17 miles further than the longest day on the Pennine Way. At least 16 hours of walking – 5 hours more than my previous best. And depending on which guide book you read, between 5,000 and 6,000 feet of ascents: equivalent to walking up Ben Nevis.

'Challenge' is an understatement. And this time I know what's coming. I know that after 23 miles on the Pennine Way I was so tired that I couldn't unfasten my boots. So let's hope I don't compound the problem by falling in another bog: I've already ticked 'walk a mile in my underpants' off the bucket list. And we'd better add 'don't fall over and break your fingers again' to the list of sensible suggestions.

What is it the Chinese say? 'A journey of a thousand miles begins with a single step.' Or as it'll be on a Saturday in July, a journey of 88,000 steps...

CHAPTER SEVENTEEN

THE BATTLE OF
WOUNDED KNEE

*My training for the Lyke Wake Walk has begun. Or
maybe not…*

"Why are you lying on the stairs, Dad?"

A-level revision clearly hadn't dimmed Alex's
powers of observation. I was indeed lying on the stairs.
And grimacing with pain.

"It's my knee."

"What about it?"

"It's gone. First when I was coming up the cliff.
And now, going upstairs. It's stopped working."

"Shall I get Mum?"

"No, no, I'll be fine. Just give me a minute."

Alex looked doubtful. "It's just that Libby's coming
round…"

Ah, the FSG. Coming round to "help me with my revision." Hadn't heard it called that before. But I could see the problem. *Come on, we'll go up to my bedroom. We can work on the causes of the First World War.* Sly grin. Wink. Another sly grin. *But you'll just need to climb over my dad first…*

"I'm going to meet her now. Try not to be there when I get back."

Thanks for the pep talk, son. But eventually a combination of hopping, crawling and tears got me to the bedroom.

"What's caused it?" my wife asked.

What hadn't caused it? "Walking. Uneven ground. Old age. Ten years of playing squash. Football. Running. Walking uphill. It's gradually chiselling away at my knee."

"Is it worth it?"

I lay on the bed with a bag of frozen peas on my left knee and considered my wife's question. For half a second.

Was walking worth it? Every time.

My later-life romance has given me some special gifts over the past 16 months: not least a sun tan and a whole new wardrobe. And socks.

Yep, socks. Never again will the family wonder what to buy me. It's Father's Day in two weeks and I can't wait. Three new pairs of walking socks. Yes, I know it's sad – erotically aroused by a pair of double-layer 1,000 mile socks – but you know how it is. A man reaches a certain stage in life…

And my new wardrobe. When I opened the wardrobe door in January 2016 75% of my clothes sniggered: they openly mocked me. Trousers that wouldn't meet round my waist? The button and the hole were in different postcodes. Now they're queuing up to be worn. Although there is one slight disadvantage. Yes, I have a 'new' wardrobe, but it largely consists of clothes bought in the 90s. "Been shopping at Oxfam again, Dad? Or did you mug a beggar…"

Then there's my tan. My distinctly uneven tan. I wear different shorts on different days – so my legs look like a Dulux colour chart running from Spice Beige through Timber Tan to Mocha Madness. But when you're walking round North Yorkshire in April and someone says, "Who's been to Tenerife then?" you know you're doing something right.

No question, walking has been good to me. But now it had sent the bill.

A quick trawl round the internet confirmed my diagnosis. Overuse. 'Your kneecap isn't tracking properly.' The prescription was simple. Use ice, strengthen the muscles round my knee and I should be able to go back to walking in six weeks' time.

But that was impossible.

Seven weeks today Alex and I are attempting the Lyke Wake Walk. Forty miles west to east across the highest, widest part of the North York Moors. I need to be fit. I need to lose some more weight. Six weeks on the sofa with the frozen peas is simply not an option.

I'd always known it would come to this: ever since I saw a 'proper walker' on the Cleveland Way.

I sighed and tapped *knee support for walking* into Amazon. A quarter of a million results. Clearly I wasn't the only person who'd spent a day face down on the stairs. And a spectacular range of prices: £8.99 up to – blimey – what looked like an entirely new knee for £115.

Or I could have 'ultimate performance knee support' for the bargain basement price of twelve quid.

I reluctantly clicked on it.

Reluctantly because I hate that about the internet. Express a mild interest, click on something and ads start stalking you. Now I'd have knee supports knocking on my virtual door for three weeks.

But look on the bright side I told myself. At least it wasn't a hernia…

SUFFERING FOR MY ART

Meanwhile, I'd finally finished 'Father, Son and the Pennine Way.' All I needed now was a book cover...

Monday. The day of the photo-shoot. I ignored my son's cheap jibes about plastic surgery and changed into my shorts. Hello, old friends. Last seen hanging on a gate to dry out after I carelessly fell into a bog.

And not really what I wanted to be wearing on a very cold, very windy day in March. Especially as we were heading for the most exposed hillside in a 20 mile radius.

But 'suffering for your art' and all that. And here was Paul Anthony Wilson, friend, ace photographer and a man wearing enough Arctic survival gear for three expeditions.

"All set?"

"Think so. Two backpacks, two pairs of walking boots, flask, sandwich, map, headphones…"

Let me explain. Last year Alex and I went for a walk on the Pennine Way: 5 days and 90 miles. And I've finally finished the book. But the photos we took – yes, even the one of me striding manfully along in my underpants (see above: bog) – have been deemed inadequate.

Jamie the Book Cover muttered something about 'definition' and 'pixels' and ordered me to engage a professional. And Paul promptly gave me a shopping list.

"We can do this in one of two ways. Either you and Alex together. Or something symbolic. Big backpack, little backpack."

"We only took one backpack." And I decided to keep quiet about who carried it for 90% of the time.

"And accessories. Something to show he's a teenager." I duly made a giant ham sandwich and stole my wife's bright orange headphones.

And here we were in the wilderness. Bleak, beautiful – and starting to rain. "Brilliant," Paul said. "Even more authentic."

Fortunately the wind was so strong the rain blew over almost before it had arrived. And I made the cowardly decision to keep my waterproof trousers on. Authenticity was one thing: dying of exposure was quite another.

"Go and stand down there," Paul said, indicating the most desolate spot he could find. But he was right, the Siberian tundra was a perfect background.

Paul's general idea was that we'd hold the map. There'd be father/son tension: one of us – no prizes for guessing – determined to go in completely the wrong direction. Ordnance Survey maps are tricky little brutes at the best of times. In a howling wind with frozen fingers they're impossible.

But not as impossible as the father/son backpack combination. However we positioned them they blew over. And damn it, I'd weighted them down before we left home. That's to say, I'd grabbed all the dirty washing and stuffed it into the backpacks. In retrospect, an imaginative way to end a marriage…

Half my underwear is missing. Do you know what happened to it?

Well, you see. I needed to weigh down the backpacks. For the photo-shoot. Realism, you understand. So I used the dirty washing. Then they blew over and, er, I hadn't fastened them properly. Er…

So my knickers are blowing across the North York Moors?

…And an interesting claim on the buildings and contents insurance.

With the still life refusing to co-operate the final choice came down to two. A photo of us holding the map and more or less looking in opposite directions.

Or Alex bounding up some stone steps with me stumbling/falling in his wake.

My focus group on Facebook were in no doubt. *Both great but 100% falling down* was one reply, neatly capturing the general mood.

But then there was a reply from Florida: *I don't like that one. The young man looks rather cruel. It looks like he is abandoning his father. And why has the old man's knee collapsed so dramatically?*

Old man? Old man? Let's hope Specsavers open a branch in Orlando pretty damn quickly. But supposing other people saw it like that? The decision was made.

And the more I looked at the other photo the more right it seemed. A ruggedly handsome father, pointing the way to his hopelessly lost son.

Strangely, most people seem to see it the other way round…

CHAPTER NINETEEN

THE RUSSIAN SPY

Three weeks until Alex and I attempt the Lyke Wake Walk. And the sun's shining. So instead of the cliff top why don't I do a dress rehearsal…

"I'm going up on the Moors," I said to my wife. "Walking some of the route. East to west, at least as far as Fylingdales. Maybe over the Pickering road as well."

"Do you need the map?" she said.

"What?" I scoffed. "I know the Moors like the back of my hand."

"Remember Alex isn't with you to navigate. Don't go wandering off course."

"For goodness sake," I said. "Stop worrying. What could possibly go wrong?"

Five words which seem to define my career as a walker…

I loaded my backpack with a month's supply of Kendal Mint Cake and jumped in the car. Ten miles up the A171 to the lay-by. Ten miles to solitude – and the silence you only truly experience when you're walking.

I'd never expected to see the Lilla Cross again. I'd thought that Sunday morning with Alex – the Sunday we came face-to-face with one of my ancestors – had been a one-off. But here I was again at the oldest Christian burial site in England: the burial place of Lilla, who died in 626 saving the life of Edwin, King of Northumbria, and was now gazing out across the North York Moors for eternity.

Time to press on. There was the road that ran around the perimeter of Fylingdales: down there in the distance was the Whitby to Pickering road. What was it? A mile? So all I had to do was find the route of the Lyke Wake Walk and follow it. And then across the road and see what we'd face in three weeks' time.

At this point a 'memo to self' might be appropriate. Remember the saying. Those that do not learn from history are doomed to repeat it.

And what had I learned from history: specifically from last year on the Pennine Way? If a gate is locked and bloody difficult to open it's probably not a good idea to climb over it and carry on walking.

But Alex – a.k.a. common sense – was at home revising for his A-levels. So my train of thought was simple. *Here I am, there's the road I need to get to, this moorland road looks like it leads there, I just need to climb over this gate…*

There were some flags that seemed to be marking a route – maybe 200 yards off to my right, but… Well, I was on a road and it was going in more or less the right direction, so let's keep going. And there's no-one in sight, so let's have a wee as well. I unbuttoned my shorts and sighed with relief…

Call of nature answered, I looked up. There was a sign in front of me. How had I not noticed it? Rusty and with a couple of holes – like the signs outside Greek villages that are periodically used for target practice – but still very definitely legible.

This is a prohibited place within the meaning of the Official Secrets Act. Any unauthorised person entering the area will be arrested and prosecuted.

Blimey, that sounded a bit draconian. I must be right on the edge of Fylingdales. Ah well, press on. Not that far to the Pickering road. And then there was another sign. Less rusty. Not been used for target practice. And saying exactly the same thing.

Then there was another one.

And it slowly dawned on James Bond that he might actually be *inside* Fylingdales. That climbing over the gate might not have been sensible. That the flags 200 yards to the right might have been trying to tell me something. That the watchers inside RAF Fylingdales, part of our National Missile Defence system, might have taken their eyes off the Kremlin for a minute…

Intruder inside the perimeter, sir
Description?
Looks like a grey-haired, middle-aged walker
Exactly what you'd expect a Russian spy to look like
Good God!
What is it, corporal?
With respect, sir, he's pissing on our perimeter sign
Pissing on our British way of life, you mean. Shoot
to kill. The Russians will deny all knowledge of him...

On reflection I'd probably gone far enough for one day. I casually strolled back to the gate. The cameras might be watching me. I very conspicuously unwrapped some Kendal Mint Cake. "I think I have a stone in my walking boot," I said out loud for the benefit of the microphones.

Maybe I shouldn't have recounted the story over dinner. It was all the proof Beverley and Alex needed.

"You'd better not let him out on his own again, Mum..."

"Not unless we want to be posting bail. I remember seeing a story on the news," she added. "A British tourist on holiday had cycled into Saddam Hussein's nuclear bunker." She shook her head slowly. "I thought to myself. 'How can anyone be that stupid...'"

CHAPTER TWENTY

THE LETTER

It hadn't been a good week.

The Grim Reaper had been rooting around in my generation.

Beverley's brother's best friend: 'make the most of the time you've got left.' And then the mother of one of Eleanor's friends: the funeral's on Tuesday.

Meanwhile Alex and I were out walking. Training for our attempt on the Lyke Wake Walk. Beverley had very kindly decanted us on the North York Moors, 13 miles from home. The only way back was to walk. And talk, as we always did.

We'd done Brexit and the General Election. Now we were in much darker territory. I'd shared the news with Alex.

"You'll still be around though, Dad," he said.

"Count on it," I said.

"At least for four more years. Just in case my essays need checking while I'm at university."

I might have shed a tear at that point. July, August, a week or so of September and he'll be gone.

But he had an even more pressing appointment. His last A-level exam in three days' time. An hour and a half of philosophy, hand his text books in and that was Alex – and us – done with school. Twenty years after Dan first went to nursery and we were finally finished. Nothing lasts for ever.

"Do you remember David Smith?" I said. "Friend of Dan's when he was in nursery?"

A stupid question, as my son wasn't slow to point out. "Was I even born when Dan was in nursery?"

"Only just. Anyway, his parents live there." I pointed down the road. "The house next to the church. I saw his dad the other day. In the hospital. When they were giving up on my finger. He didn't look well at all. Thought I should invite him out for a drink."

"What? Just in case?"

"Well… I like the guy."

"Have you ever invited him out for a drink before?"

"No. I've played golf with him though."

"When?"

"Ten years ago."

"So a sudden invitation might come as something of a surprise?"

I could see Alex's point. But when the man with the scythe is scrolling through your contacts list you have to do something. Fortunately my son had the answer.

"You should write him a letter."

"That's a tough one. Thought I'd just drop you a line – in case you died…"

"No, I was reading Christopher Hitchens…" Ah, the gospel according to Hitch. Alex is a fully paid up member. "…He says that if you're in any doubt about writing someone a letter then you should. It's bound to make at least one of you feel better."

"Yeah, I can see that."

And I could. A postcard maybe. *Walking past your house the other day. Reminded me I haven't seen you for a while. Hope you're well.*

Or at least, better than the last time I saw you…

"How far do you think it will be?"

"Until we're home? 12, maybe 13 miles," I said. "4½ hours or so."

Alex shrugged. No problem.

But I had another moment of doubt. The Lyke Wake Walk was 40 miles. When I was young and fit I got into the London Marathon twice. Both times I injured myself and couldn't do it. And gradually my youth and fitness crumbled in the face of the passing years – and their allies, the cheeseboard and the wine bottle.

All that changed when Beverley gave me a Fitbit. The Pennine Way last year, the Lyke Wake Walk this year. But 40 miles in one day? It might be several thousand steps too far.

"But what's the alternative?" I said out loud. "You've got to challenge yourself. Go outside your comfort zone. Better to fail than not to try."

We were walking past the church. Alex paused and put his hand on my shoulder. "Good for you, Dad. It'll be a while before anyone sends you a letter…"

CHAPTER TWENTY-ONE

I SUBMIT TO MY WIFE

My wife sighed. "Come on then," she said. "If I have to. Take your trousers off and lie on the bed. It's only small. It won't take long."

When a woman says that you've no choice. I unfastened my jeans and did as I was told.

"Right," my wife said.

"Don't hurt me…"

"Maybe. Move your leg. Let me try and find it."

I should apologise at this point. Sorry if you think you've stumbled across Fifty Shades of Married Life. I had an acrochordon, or fibroepithelial polyp – and it was in my groin.

What? Oh alright, if you want to trivialise my suffering. I had a skin tag.

It was big. And irritating. And it got caught on everything. Especially when I was out walking. It was like having a particularly ferocious gnat living in my trousers.

Meanwhile my wife – whose eyes light up when there is a chance of performing surgery on me – was rummaging in her sewing box. She produced a pair of scissors. Big ones.

I hadn't realised she had a sideline gelding horses.

"You're not going to use those on me?"

"I will do if you don't keep still."

"Do you want me to hold it?"

"No. Just get your hands out of the way. I'll use my sewing scissors. It's only a skin tag. And it's turned black."

I'd finally realised I needed to do something about the tag when I started walking like John Wayne. Hot weather made the damn thing especially sore. Walking uphill in the July heatwave? The Spanish Inquisition would have approved.

I called on Dr. Google. Goodness knows why you can't see your GP for three weeks when Google can diagnose most things in five minutes. Let Google write prescriptions and NHS waiting lists would disappear overnight.

But for once the good doctor from California didn't dispense any words of comfort. Instead I was terrified – all thanks to a thread on *Mumsnet*. It was encouragingly called, *Decided to do a DIY Jobby on my Skin Tag*.

I had watched my wife give birth three times and it had given me the vague suspicion that women are tougher than men – tougher than this man anyway. The thread on Mumsnet confirmed it.

Tweezers, nail clippers, kitchen scissors. There was nothing these women hadn't done. I awarded Spartan of the Year to the mum who simply anaesthetised herself with gin and pulled it off.

None of that for me, mate. I phoned the doctors. Three weeks? In your dreams: the first appointment with my own GP clashed with the next appearance of Haley's Comet. But I could see the locum – a man who proved that passing the 'bedside manner' module wasn't essential in a medical degree.

"I can tie it up with string," he said. "Eventually it'll turn black and drop off. Might throb for a bit mind you." Given that walking like John Wayne had given way to walking like someone with acute diarrhoea it seemed a small price to pay.

I spent a very pleasant weekend limping around with six inches of NHS string dangling from my groin. Surprisingly, a celibate weekend…

But eventually the wretched thing cooperated and turned black. But it refused to fall off. At which point I decided that home surgery was the only option and removed my trousers.

"Be gentle. You know I can't stand pain."

"I know you're a hopeless wimp. I know that if you'd been giving birth we'd have had one child, not three. Right, here goes…"

"Aaaagggghhhh!" I yelled. But it was off.

The bedroom door opened and a teenage head appeared. The Beloved Daughter. "I heard you tell Dad to take his trousers off. Then he started moaning. You're not…"

"No," I said. "We're not. Now go and do your homework." She'd learn. There were some things in married life that were even more basic than sex…

CHAPTER TWENTY-TWO

COLD FEET ABOUT
WET FEET

"How do you fancy spending Monday evening in a bog?"

"This is obviously leading somewhere, Dad…"

"For once, yes. We're doing the Lyke Wake Walk on Saturday."

"I know that."

"So as the army say, 'time spent in reconnaissance is never wasted.' I think we should go and walk through the boggy section. See how boggy it really is."

Alex consulted Libby. She was working on Monday night. So reconnaissance was fine.

And here we were. An hour's drive and our boots on. "Sixty minutes in one direction. Turn round, come back. That'll give us a good idea of what we're going to face on Saturday."

The sun was beating down: probably the hottest day of the year. Alex set off in front of me, literally bouncing across the peat. It was like watching a small child on a trampoline.

I set off after him. Trampoline? I was Neil Armstrong, bouncing across the moon.

How easy was this going to be? All we had to do was walk 20 miles and then we'd have springs on our feet.

And then an old friend tapped me on the shoulder. The old familiar trickle of water into my boot.

"Alex..."

"What, Dad?"

"I'm sinking."

And for the next five hundred yards we were wading through the bog, sinking up to our ankles. Then we were back on dry land. Then into another bog.

Not an hour of walking on the moon: an hour of jumping from one island of terra firma to the next, of listening to my boots ominously squelching and wondering if there was a towel in the car.

There was – and mercifully some water. Plenty of it.

"Maybe if it's this hot all week the bogs will dry out," I said.

Alex looked doubtful. "I think it's water coming up from below. Not down from above…"

It was all academic.

Two days later I was sitting in my office.

In my underpants.

My last serious lunchtime walk before the big day and the heavens had opened – obviously when I was at the far end of the beach. My clothes now hung soggily from the cupboard door as I tapped diligently away at a client's blog.

Yes, the door was locked. Well, I think it was…

Mid-afternoon and the rain was still hammering against the office window. And I had more pressing concerns than a pair of soggy chinos. According to the BBC weather map – I was going to need a new 'refresh' key in a minute – it was raining even harder over the Moors.

Memories of last year and the Pennine Way floated back. Soaked to the skin, slipping and sliding over the wet rocks and loose stones. Walking up tracks that had suddenly become streams. Hawes to Tan Hill – the day I wouldn't have survived without my son – had been 17 miles: the Lyke Wake Walk was 40.

I took my cold feet home with me. "Do you think we should postpone it? Give the bogs time to dry out?"

"But how do we know it won't rain then as well?"

Alex had a point. And there weren't that many alternatives. "We can't do it next weekend. Mum wants to do a car boot sale. August 5th maybe? Except that's the day before Ellie's birthday. And there's a limit to how many Saturdays you can have off work. August 12th? It's starting to get dark. August 19th you've just had your A-level results. August 26th? Bank holiday weekend? Just before you go to university. Is that possible?"

"No," my wife said. "I'm going to a wedding." So that was that. No-one to meet us at half-way with sandwiches: so no walk.

"We need to do it this weekend, Dad."

"I just don't want to get soaked again, Alex. I was emotionally scarred by Hawes to Tan Hill. Isn't there another window in the weather?"

"'Window in the weather?' We're not climbing Everest, Dad."

"Why are you so adamant?"

"Because I've just had my hair cut. I like my hair short when I'm walking."

He'd had a haircut. On such whims are the fates of nations decided.

Should we not postpone the attack, great Caesar? The omens are not favourable.

Nay, Brutus. Call the men to arms. I've had my hair cut specially.

So on Saturday we go to Osmotherley to walk 40 miles across the highest, widest part of the North York Moors. Cometh the hour, cometh the men. And according to the weather forecast, the men will be wet…

CHAPTER TWENTY-THREE

THE FROG ON THE MOOR

4:50 in the morning. Saturday July 22nd. Our attempt on the Lyke Wake Walk begins…

Alex and I left the B&B and started walking. Today was the day: the Lyke Wake Walk. And for Formula 1 fans, we were starting in 'full wets:' waterproof jacket, trousers and – never say never – gaiters. (Google them if you're not sure. You won't find a more erotic piece of clothing on the planet.)

For fans of BBC weather maps the rain was light blue. There was plenty of dark blue forecast as well. And some green. What was that? Thunderstorms? And one of the dark green blobs had a white circle in the centre of it. The apocalypse, probably…

"It'll be fine," I said with more confidence than I felt, as we walked the two miles from the B&B to the official start of the Walk. Memo to self: if you are walking 40 miles adding two on at the beginning isn't a brilliant idea…

"That *must* be it," I said three hours later. "I know all the hills are in the first ten miles but there can't be any more."

"Just one more, Dad…"

Second memo to self. Maybe train with a backpack in future?

What was in my backpack? Waterproofs, water, Kendal Mint Cake, pyjamas from last night, toothbrush. And, by the time I'd hauled myself up Hasty Bank, a couple of house bricks.

I gasped my now-familiar phrase. "Don't let me slow you down. Wait for me at the top."

This was the most climbing I'd ever done in a day. More than the first day on the Pennine Way and I simply wasn't fit enough. What was I? A stone heavier than last year? Plus the weight of the bricks…

But finally we were at the top and on an old – and flat – railway line. And the sun had come out. Waterproofs off, shorts on for the rest of the day. Just six easy miles along here and Bev would be waiting for us with lunch. And I'd be fully recovered…

"It's sunny down there," Alex said, pointing down into a distant valley, "But…"

I looked to my left. The clouds were closing in. Was that a spot of rain? "It'll be just a passing shower," I said.

Which brings me neatly to the story of the frog…

Is it true? Is it urban myth? You pop a frog into a pan of water and gradually increase the heat. That was me last Saturday. The Frog on the Moor. An exact parallel…

Hmmm… Someone's put me in a pan of water

Well, here I am in my shorts but it's looking a bit cloudy

What's that? Is the water getting warmer? Maybe…

In fact it's starting to rain. Maybe it'll soon stop…

The water is getting warmer. Ah well…

Nope, it's raining harder. And I'm starting to get wet. Ah well, I'll dry when the sun comes out

Blimey, you'd almost say this water was hot

Actually it's pouring down. And I'm getting soaked

Did I say hot? It's- At which point our urban myth frog departs this life.

"Can you just stop a minute?" I asked Alex. And then I attempted mission impossible.

Here you go, should you choose to accept it…

You are soaking wet. The rain is lashing down. There is nothing to sit on. You have to get into a pair of waterproof trousers. You do this by pulling them over your boots. But you can't. Because your boots are wet. You're hopping around to keep your balance. The only solution is to take a boot off. But you can't do that because now it's lashing down even harder. So you hop around in the middle of the North York Moors with a pair of waterproof trousers dangling uselessly from one of your boots. While your son – who never took his waterproofs off – looks on and wonders how he can possibly be related to this idiot.

"£\$%& it," you say eventually. "The sun will come out in a minute."

It doesn't. Lashing down gives way to hammering down. The rain is just torrential. Come hell or high water – and it's going to be the latter and pretty damn quickly – I have to get those waterproof trousers on. "Stand still," I say again. "Hold me up."

The definition of stupid was not putting my waterproofs on when it first started to rain. The definition of whatever comes after stupid is what I did next. I needed to bend down to get the trousers over my foot. And I needed to take my soaking wet shorts off.

I did it without thinking, without checking the direction of the rain. I'm sorry for the mental image but I pulled my shorts off and pointed my bum straight into the rain.

Bluntly it would be a tragic waste if I didn't become famous. *I'm a Celebrity?* Bring it on. 'All you've got to do is get your trousers on while we pour gallons of water down your underpants.'

'No problem, Ant. Already done it on the Moors, mate.'

"You can probably file that under 'bad decisions,' Dad," Alex said five minutes later.

"What?"

"Taking your shorts off and pointing your bum at the rain."

He was right. But it was getting increasingly difficult to tell what he was saying – because he was five, 10, 20 yards in front of me. I couldn't keep up. It was time to admit what I'd first realised at the top of Hasty Bank. I wasn't going to finish. The hills and the rain had beaten me.

"Alex," I shouted through the rain.

He stopped and waited for me.

"What is it?"

"I'm not going to be able to do this. We're two hours behind schedule. We're not going to finish until midnight. And what the hell are the bogs going to be like after this?"

'Don't get hung up on finishing,' Bev had said. 'Just enjoy the time with Alex. Even if you don't finish the walk you've still spent time with your son.'

But when you're the dad: when you've said, 'We should do a walk every year' and you've pestered him to choose one… Then saying 'I'm not going to finish' doesn't come easily.

"I'm really sorry," I said. "I didn't want to let you down."

Not for the first time in our relationship I wondered which one of us was the adult. "We can come back next year, Dad. The Lyke Wake Walk isn't going anywhere."

And neither am I – as long as I have my son to walk with…

CHAPTER TWENTY-FOUR

7 MORE THINGS WALKING HAS GIVEN ME

So we didn't manage to do the Lyke Wake Walk. I spent the rest of the summer feeling that I'd let Alex down: but finally I managed a sense of perspective…

Christmas 2015. My wife gives me a Fitbit. It demands I do 10,000 steps a day. What? My first day yields just 3,874 steps. Clearly I have no hope of ever reaching 10,000 in a day.

But gradually I make changes – and one day I'm walking past the Art Gallery and my Fitbit has an orgasm on my wrist. Buzzing, vibrating, getting excited: there's no other word to describe it. Soon after that I have to admit it: I've fallen in love with walking.

Eighteen months on and — as I write — on my 175th consecutive day of 10,000 or more steps, walking has been a generous lover. I've already discussed my tan, my slightly-worrying erotic attachment to walking socks and my new wardrobe. Here are seven other things the affair has given me…

1. **A different view of the world.** I love this about walking. You see the world from a different angle. There's a village up the road from us. I must have driven through it a thousand times. Suddenly I'm walking along an old railway track that runs behind the village. And I see it from a different angle. I never realised there was a farm right in the middle of the village. All you see from the road is the house. See it from the back and there's an enormous duck pond. And then I'm looking inland at the Moors, when I've spent my life looking across them and out to sea. There are some spectacular and beautiful views in the UK, but sometimes there is only one way to see them. And that way is to walk.

2. **The whole world** – OK, there are some countries I'll draw the line at. But walking through Northern Spain? A gentle jaunt from Bologna to Florence? The length of New Zealand? Bring it on: who wants to lie on a beach?

3. **A commitment to my own health.** I was critically ill in the spring of 2006. "This tablet, that tablet, you'd better take some of these as well. And this one." "How long for?" I asked. "Well, the rest of your life, obviously." In Autumn 2015 I threw them all away and started walking. The entire country needs a prescription for walking boots.

4. **Determination**. The middle day of our walk on the Pennine Way was from Hawes to the Tan Hill Inn. 17 miles in torrential rain and a waterproof jacket that wasn't. A day that my son pulled me through. If something is difficult now I just mutter "Hawes to Tan Hill" and get on with it.

5. **The future** – I'm angry with myself for discovering walking so late in life. I'm angry about the sunrises and the spaces I've missed, the holidays in Northumberland where I've been so close to a National Trail but didn't even know what a National Trail was. But now, I will simply walk until I'm no longer capable. We've all got to go sometime and if that's one Sunday morning when I'm walking on the cliff top, the spring sun glinting off the North Sea… Well, I'll settle for that.

6. **The best father/son time of my life.** In those five days on the Pennine Way I was frightened, I was soaked, I fell in a bog, I fell over again an hour later and broke two fingers – and it was the best father/son time of my life.

7. **Sex** – and I must apologise for this last one, gentle reader – but blimey. More energy, more stamina, flat stomach. What's not to love about walking...

It's Saturday June 2nd. I'm just finishing the book and I'm now on 504 consecutive days of 10,000 steps. I tell you, this walking lark can become addictive...

CHAPTER TWENTY-FIVE

TOENAIL CLIPPINGS

*Originally written in early February 2018. Just before
my wife suggested I move into the garage…*

"I should have done it years ago," I admitted.

"You would have done if you'd listened to my advice."

I didn't reply. I knew my wife was right. She knew she was right. No doubt she'd be sneaking up to the bedroom and writing it down in the remind-him-of-this-in-20-years notebook that all wives keep.

What were we discussing? My feet.

My feet which – after a lifetime of football, squash, running and now walking – are not hugely attractive. There must be a woman somewhere in the world who's turned on by men's feet, but it certainly isn't my wife. At least, not by my feet. As a general rule she likes to keep at least a postcode between her and any sight of my toes.

Until a couple of weeks ago. "I really need you to look at this toenail," I said.

"Why?"

"It's growing vertically."

"If I must." She took a stiff drink of gin and put her reading glasses on.

"It's disgusting," she said. "You need to see someone."

"It's damaged," I said in my defence. "I did it last year on the Lyke Wake Walk. Can you just try and trim it a bit?"

Greater love hath no woman. Lady Macbeth screwed her courage to the sticking place and reached for the nail clippers.

"That's the best I can do," she said five minutes later. "You *definitely* need to see someone."

So I did. Finally. I sighed and tapped 'chiropodist' into Google. Another concession to the advancing years…

…Which was something I shared with the man now bending over my bare feet. "I'm just waiting for an appointment," Tim said. "Two new hips. Having them both done at the same time."

Compared to which a vertical toenail seemed insignificant. But there were other problems.

"Well," he said, "I've seen worse. You've got two decent toenails."

Two out of ten. Hardly a pass mark.

He started clipping. And bemoaning the march of progress. "Toenail clippings," he said. "Doctors don't ask for them any more. Rely on blood samples these days."

"I thought it was only Macbeth's witches that wanted toenail clippings. You know, to go with the eye of newt…"

"Should still use them," Tim said. "You can tell a lot about a man from his toenail clippings," he added ominously.

Goodness knows what they were telling him about me. But by the time he'd finished clipping, filing and grinding my feet looked better. A lot better.

"You've got a lot of hard skin," Tim said. "Probably an infection. Too much time in trainers."

"What should I do about it?"

"You need to bathe your feet once a week. Do it while you're watching TV. That's what I do."

"Just in warm water?"

"No, no, no. That's not going to do it. Warm water, salt and vinegar."

I took a long time to drive home that night. I stopped a couple of times to rehearse the conversation. *So you see, darling, what he recommends – while we're watching TV together – is that I sit with my feet in a bowl of warm water, salt and vinegar. Yes, it might smell a bit. Yes, in the lounge, darling.*

As I say, I rehearsed the conversation several times. So here I am, sitting at the dining room table on Friday night. On my own. Writing. With my feet in a bowl of water...

And looking at Amazon. Tim said I should buy a toenail grinder. Or 'electric pedicure kit' as they're more correctly called. I can get it tomorrow with Prime. Why not? Is there a better way to spend a weekend?

And according to Amazon it's 'a great Valentine's Day gift.'

Thanks for the advice. But I'll stick with flowers...

CHAPTER TWENTY-SIX

HERE WE GO AGAIN

*Written – with a great deal of pleasure – in April
2018*

"So Mum will drive us up to Edinburgh," I said to
Alex, "We'll collect you at the end of term, 40-odd
miles to Glasgow and then you and I walk the West
Highland Way."

"Sounds good."

It sounded good to me too. Better than good. Two
years after our five days on the Pennine Way Alex and
I were off again, and this time we were invading
Scotland. 92 miles of the West Highland Way from
Glasgow to Fort William, the most beautiful National
Trail in the UK.

"Loch Lomond," I said. "Glencoe, Ben Nevis…
Aye, wee man. I cannae wait."

My wife coughed.

"Sorry," I said. "I'll try to curb my inner William Wallace until we're actually in Scotland."

My wife coughed again.

"Oh," I said. "Right. That is … darling … would you mind awfully, driving us to Glasgow?"

"And then driving home on my own."

"Well, yes. Sorry."

"And how do you propose to get home from Fort William? Do you know how far it is to Fort William?"

I had a feeling I was going to find out quite quickly…

"342 miles."

I mumbled something about looking at train times. But I needn't have worried. However much I wanted Scotland, Scotland didn't want me.

"A twin room? For the one night in June? Och, no. We're fully booked right through to September."

"You're walking the West Highland Way? Aye, well, so is everyone else, I'm afraid."

"June? I'm afraid not. We do have a wee bothy you could use. It does nae have any water, mind…"

No room at the inn and no room at the B&Bs. All the fault of the tour companies, who buy up all the rooms. See above, the most beautiful – and popular – National Trail in the UK.

Time for Plan B. "And preferably one that doesn't involve me driving to Vladivostok," my wife said.

Various Plan B's were considered. "The South Downs Way?" Our road manager raised an eyebrow.

"Somewhere in Wales?" She raised two eyebrows.

"Lady Anne Clifford," I said.

"Who?"

"She was born in Skipton Castle and died in Brougham Castle, near Penrith. In 1676," I added helpfully. "Now there's a walk named after her."

"From Skipton to Penrith?" Alex said. "We've already done that."

He was right. Lady Anne sounded suspiciously like Pennine Way Lite. There was a thought at the back of my mind. For some reason I didn't want to voice it.

Fortunately my son did. "Why don't we pick up where we left off?"

"In Dufton?"

"Yep. And walk to the end. In Scotland."

So that's what we're going to do. The B&Bs are booked and on Monday July 16th it will be 'Return to the Pennine Way.'

Or 'Pennine Way, the sequel.'

'The Pennine Way Strikes Back?'

Whatever we call it, we'll start in Dufton and six days later we'll arrive at the Border Hotel in Kirk Yetholm, the official end of the Pennine Way and a mile inside the border.

So we *will* invade Scotland. But only just…

My wife was confused. "Let me get this straight," she said. "You started the Pennine Way by walking the middle section. Now you're doing the end…"

She had a point. But whatever order Alex and I were doing it in, we were doing it together. Two years ago we'd walked up the hill into Dufton, finished our five days and committed to another walk. But I'd had my doubts. A-levels, university, the First Serious Girlfriend. Would he really want to spend another week with his dad?

Now I had my answer.

"Twin room? July 18th? No problem. We'll look forward to seeing you."

Not as much as I'll look forward to seeing you…

CHAPTER TWENTY-SEVEN

'FATHER, SON AND THE PENNINE WAY'

As I mentioned earlier, half a dozen of the stories in this book are from the summer of 2016, when Alex and I spent five days walking 90 miles on the Pennine Way – the UK's toughest National Trail.

In this book I've left that story as we set off from Malham on the morning of August 1st. The five days that followed were quite simply five of the best days of my life. They didn't quite go according to plan – to say there were one or two mishaps is a major understatement – but I wouldn't have changed a thing. Despite the fact that I can now no longer make a fist with my left hand…

If you'd like to read the full story, the book is available on Amazon, for both the Kindle and in paperback.

You can find it on your local Amazon store by typing this into your browser: books2read.com/pennineway

And people seem to like it. I've been overwhelmed by the comments, reviews and feedback I've received. Reviews on Amazon include:

"A fantastic laugh out loud read that will appeal to both walkers and non-walkers. Mark's wonderful relationship with his son shines through."

"Once I started I couldn't put the book down and lived every step with the author and his son. Can't wait for his next book…"

"I read travel books all the time but this one is different. I was hooked from the start and laughed out loud many times."

"Couldn't put this book down. I was almost laughing out loud and in tears of emotion at the same time. The best book I have read for a long time."

"What a great read! The book is informative, funny and – as a parent – emotional."

"Enjoyable, funny, informative, heartfelt, relaxing and impossible to put down. The best book I've read for a while."

BOOK REVIEWS

Thank you for reading *Walking Shorts*. I really hope you enjoyed it.

If you did, could I ask a favour? Would you please review the book on Amazon? Go to the following link to do this: books2read.com/walkingshorts

Reviews are important: first and foremost they help to sell the book. Secondly, there are some review and book promotion sites that will only look at a book if it has a certain number of reviews and/or a certain ratio of 5* reviews. Lastly, reviews convince Amazon's algorithm – the deity all writers now pray to – that you are a writer to be taken seriously: that it might be worth Amazon's while to recommend you to other readers.

So I'd really appreciate you taking five minutes to leave a review, and thank you in advance to anyone who does so.

WHAT NEXT?

Father, Son and Return to the Pennine Way

The lure of the Pennine Way proved irresistible – and this year Alex and I picked up where we left off. On Monday July 16th we set off from Dufton to walk the last 100 miles to Kirk Yetholm in Scotland.

I'm now writing the book about those six days and the Kindle version will be published on November 16th 2018. You can order it at: www.amazon.co.uk/dp/B07JKMQNF3 and – if you order before November 16th – it will be delivered as soon as it's published.

Rest assured that this year's walk was just as eventful – and funny – as the one you've just read about. And yes, once again we met a colourful cast of characters…

But there were changes as well. Both of us were two years older. Inevitably, our father/son relationship had altered slightly…

After that my intention is to publish my full series of 'Best Dad' books, covering 15 years and more than 500,000 words of family life. There will be seven books in total, and I will start to publish these early in

2019. If you'd like a sneak preview, there is a sample book available on Amazon: here's the link www.amazon.co.uk/dp/B008EM5DCQ

And yes, Alex and I will be lacing up our boots again in the summer of 2019.

In the meantime, if you'd like to receive regular updates on my writing, including previews, short stories and exclusive content, you can join my mailing list here: www.subscribepage.com/markrichards

ACKNOWLEDGEMENTS

A brief word of thanks to those virtual friends who were kind enough to read an early draft of this book and find the inevitable typos and mistakes. Your help is very much appreciated – but sadly you can now look forward to a string of similar requests…

And specific thanks to two people who now seem to be integral to my writing career. Firstly thank you to Kevin Partner, my tech guru, who does all the things I simply do not understand but without which there'd be no book.

And secondly to Paul Wilson, who once again was hauled out onto a desolate moor for the cover photo. Although I am starting to be slightly wary when Paul says, "I've had an idea…"

THAT'S IT…

…I've just about reached my 20,000 word limit. Thank you again for reading the book – and if you'd like to connect with me online, here are my contact details:

W   www.markrichards.co.uk

T   @BestDadICanBe

F   www.facebook.com/MarkRichardsAuthor/

ABOUT THE AUTHOR

Ask any writer what their most difficult piece of writing is and the answer is always the same: writing about yourself. It's more or less impossible: as the old saying goes, you just stare at a blank piece of paper until your forehead starts to bleed.

But it has to be done, so here goes…

I spent most of my working life in the financial services industry: nice suits, plenty of clients and 14 stripy ties. But I always had a small voice inside me. "Let me out," it said, "I'm a writer."

Occasionally, I did let the small voice out. I had a mid-life crisis and did some stand-up comedy in my spare time, and I started writing a humorous weekly newspaper column about family life. But by and large I kept the small voice firmly under control – and I'd occasionally buy a new stripy tie to re-focus myself.

Then, in October 2009, my elder brother died of cancer. His wife asked me to deliver the eulogy. Mike had been an army officer. The crematorium – just outside Winchester – was packed with other army officers. Stiff, formal, serious. My speech was light-hearted, whimsical – full of stories about how Mike taught me to play cricket and then, as I got older, how he taught me to drink beer and chase girls (after which, cricket didn't seem quite so exciting…)

As I stood up to speak I thought I'd badly misjudged my audience. I very nearly lost my nerve. But they were laughing within twenty seconds. And as I left the crematorium, an old man – still ramrod-straight – approached me. "I was your brother's first commanding officer," he said. "Reached the age now where I go to a damn funeral every week. Best eulogy I've heard. Good man."

Those four words – 'best eulogy I've heard' – were the four words that turned me into a writer. As I drove away from the crematorium I realised that I either let the small voice out and pursued my dream – or I forgot about it for good.

Six months later I sold my business, sent my stripy ties to the charity shop, and started writing…

Printed in Great Britain
by Amazon